THE DIRTY PROFESSOR

BETH A. FREELY

THE MUSES FUNHOUSE

The Dirty Professor: Tainted Professors by

Beth A. Freely

Copyright © 2024 by Beth A. Freely

The Muses Funhouse

www.themusesfunhouse.com

Hope, New Mexico 88250

All rights reserved, including the right to reproduce this book or portions thereof in any form whatsoever. For information about this book, please contact Beth A. Freely at bethafreely@gmail.com or brauch@themusesfunhouse.com.

This book is entirely a work of fiction. The names, characters, places, and incidents depicted herein are either products of the author's imagination or are used fictitiously. Any resemblance to actual events, locales, or persons, living or dead, is entirely coincidental.

No generative artificial intelligence (AI) was used in the writing of this work. The author expressly prohibits any entity from using this publication to train technologies to generate text, including, without limitation, technologies capable of generating works in the same style or genre as this publication. The author reserves all rights to license the use of this work for generative AI training and development of machine learning language models.

Contents

Chapter One	1
Chapter Two	11
Chapter Three	21
Chapter Four	33
Chapter Five	53
Chapter Six	61
Chapter Seven	70
Chapter Eight	79
Chapter Nine	91

Chapter Ten	105
Chapter Eleven	113
Chapter Twelve	123
Chapter Thirteen	133
Resources	139
About The Author	143
Also By Beth A. Freely	145
About The Tainted Professors	147

Chapter One

"You fucking jerk. You took my time slot!"

Dr. Ivan Petrov looked up from his laptop, his fingers stilling over the keyboard. He stared at the woman standing in his office doorway, her red button-down shirt hanging untucked over her blue jeans. He loved that color on her. It set off her amber eyes and gave her pale complexion a flush. He rests his chin on his fist, a devious smile crossing his lips. "Whatever are you talking about, *dushenka*?" he asked, his voice still tinged with his native Russian accent.

Anna Cassidine stared at him and shook her head, laughing as she stepped into the room. "Oh no, you don't, Ivan. You are not going to get away with calling me 'sweetheart.' I'm pissed at you. You took my time slot. I've had that time slot for five years, and here you come, swooping in and snatching it up for your Russian literature class."

Ivan stood up and walked around his desk. He closed the door after gently tugging her in the room. "First off, I have students who can't fit the class into their schedule with the current time slot, and they need the credit. They are seniors. Do you want them to wait to graduate? No one else could swap the class except you." He grinned down at her, standing in her personal space. "So, the scheduling director swapped us out. I told her you wouldn't mind."

"Dammit, Ivan. I mind. I do mind. I mind greatly." She punched his chest. "Back up," she laughed. He had a way of invading her personal space and making her warm. "Ugh. You drive me up the wall. You could've waited until I got back from vacation and talked to me about it."

"I wasn't going to ruin your vacation. And I had a plan to make it up to you when you got back." He leaned closer to her. "Dinner tonight?"

Anna shook her head, looking away from Ivan with a chuckle. "Ivan, I swear. You have a bad habit of disarming me when I'm not prepared." She leaned back against the wall. Before she could continue, there was a knock on the door. She remained quiet as he opened the door, effectively hiding her. She listened quietly to his conversation with one of his upcoming students, folding her arms over her chest. Once he closed the door, she met his gaze. "Fine. Dinner tonight. But you're not getting my time slot after this semester."

"Oh, *dushenka*. You know that your creative writing classes and my Russian literature class go hand in hand," he teased. He stared at her. "I've missed you. How was your vacation?" Ivan leaned back on his desk, his hands gripping the edges.

Anna met his gaze. "I hate it when you get logical. I want my time slot back, and the vacation was fantastic. I've got two camera chips of photos to go through."

"Still going to share them?"

Anna walked over to him, matching his stance against his desk. "Yeah. How could I not?" She nudged him with her shoulder. They had been close friends and colleagues since college when he was still a foreign exchange student working on getting his citizenship, and she was still deciding what she wanted her degree in. He had planned to return to Russia but changed his mind, settling in New York City when he discovered they both got jobs at Columbia University.

"I think we should hit up East Harlem Bottling Company, have some pub grub and a few beers, and talk about it," Ivan suggested. He looked down at her. "What do you think?" He tugged her long brown ponytail playfully.

"All right. Meet you out front in a half hour. I need to finish up a few things in my office."

Ivan nodded. "Fair enough." He watched her leave his office, her hips swinging as she walked down the hall to her office. He returned to the document he was working on, a smile on his face.

The fare at the East Harlem Bottling Company was good, as always. Anna got the Butternut Squash soup with a variety of her favorite appetizers, while Ivan got the Jagerschnitzel. It was the closest thing to the food of his youth that he could get so far from home. They ate in silence, washing it all down with a local beer before settling in to talk.

Anna watched him. He drove her crazy with his sexy accent and neatly trimmed goatee. He was her best friend, but there was so much more under the surface. If they allowed themselves to be and give in…no, she wasn't going to let her mind wander in that direction. This was Ivan. He knew her secrets, good, bad, and ugly, and she knew his.

"So, are we going to talk about this time slot I apparently stole from you?" he finally asked.

Anna set her pint glass down, licking the remnants of her drink from her lips. "You did steal it from me, you jerk," she laughed. She held up her hands in defense. "But I get it. I'm not happy with it, but I'll figure out what to do with that time instead. The director already gave me my schedule for the classes I'm teaching, and it's not the worst thing in the world." She leaned back in her chair. "I don't get why these kids are so into Russian lit."

"That's not the first time you've said that," he stated. Ivan nodded at the waitress as she brought them another glass of beer.

"Russian literature is dark and depressing and dry," Anna defended. She had read plenty of books by Russian authors. "You know the only Russian author I can stand is Chekov."

Ivan leaned on the table. "But there are so many more. And not all of it is dark and depressing. What if I told you that some of the best Russian literature happens to be romantic and erotic and sensual," he countered.

Anna scoffed. "You mean *Lolita* by Nabakov."

"No, I don't mean *Lolita*. However, to be fair, it should be considered. There are other authors that infused their works with sexual undertones and metaphors that make their writing sensual."

Ivan was not convincing Anna. "Name one."

"Pushkin."

She shook her head. "I've never read anything by him."

Ivan slowly smiled. "Then maybe you should." He picked up his pint glass and took a drink. "Even Chekov had sexual undertones in his writing. Your favorite play by him is *Uncle Vanya*, right? Think about the character Astrov. His is the case of unrequited love."

Anna's eyes narrowed at him. "Yelena pushes him away and deflects his advances."

Like you, Ivan thought to himself. He sighed and leaned his elbows on the table, clasping his hands as he stared into his pint glass in contemplation. "Let me prove it to you then. We have two weeks before classes start again. I was going to head up to the family house in Sleepy Hollow tomorrow and take a few days to just enjoy nature. Why don't you come with me?"

Anna blinked at him. "You want me to do to Headless Horseman country and do what?"

Ivan looked up at her. "Discuss romance and erotic passages in Russian literature. Let me prove to you how sensual it is. If I haven't convinced you by the end of the week, I'll ask the director to give you back your time slot next semester."

Anna looked at him. It was a chance to get away with Ivan alone, with no students, no family, or other distractions. It was a chance to actually sit and talk and maybe, just maybe, finally tell him how she feels about him. She bit her lower lip. "And if you do convince me?"

Ivan shrugged. "I keep the spot, and we enjoy a new understanding of one another."

A new understanding of one another. How long had they been dancing around the proverbial elephant in the room? How much longer were they going to ignore what was in between them? This was Anna's chance to let him know how she felt finally. "All right. You have until we return to the city to convince me that

Russian literature is erotic, romantic, and sensual. I don't know how you plan on accomplishing this, but I'm willing to take the chance…if for no other reason than to get my time slot back." She tapped her glass against his, sealing the deal. "I don't know how you plan to do it, but I'll enjoy watching you try." She finished off her beer.

"Let's get out of here then. I'll pick you up tomorrow afternoon. Pack some hiking clothes, you know, the usual stuff you need for walks in the woods in the cooler evenings. I'll get the groceries. Be ready by three."

"Three it is." Anna picked up the check and started towards the bar. "You've got your work cut out for you, Ivan Petrov. You better make this good," she challenged.

Ivan finished his own drink and slid from the booth. He had no idea how he was going to convince her, but he could wing it until something came to mind. He liked a challenge, especially if that challenge was Anna Cassidine.

Chapter Two

"Wait. You're going to Sleepy Hollow with Ivan? To...explore Russian literature."

"That is what I said." Anna looked at her best friend, Amy, as she continued sorting out the clothes she planned to take with her. August was always a strange month in the Hudson Valley. The days could be in the 80s, while the nights could drop as low as the 50s. The Petrov family home was one of the old historic houses in Sleepy Hollow, not one of the famous ones, but one that dated back to the Revolutionary War. It was well cared for and modern, a two-story colonial that had been renovated over the years. On the outside, the red brick face still showed signs of age, but inside, it was comfortable and cozy. Anna folded a light-weight sweater and added it to her duffle bag. "It's nothing like you're thinking," she stated.

Amy harumphed. "It's exactly what I'm thinking. Ivan Petrov has been trying to get in your knickers since the two of you were first-year students in college. And you've been smitten with him since the first day he uttered his name with that heavy Russian accent." Amy stood and walked towards Anna. "I am Ivan Petrov, from Moscow," she stated, imitating Ivan. "And you are a beautiful American woman. Could you fall in love with someone like me?"

Anna stared at Amy. "Your accent is terrible. You need to lower the pitch of your voice. Make it a little gruffer."

"Like this?" Amy asked, suddenly sounding like Dolph Lundgren. "I will take you down, Rocky Balboa."

It was enough to send Anna into a fit of giggles. She lightly pushed Amy away from her when her friend started making kissing noises at her. "I assure you, it's all academic. He made a bet with me that he could prove to me that Russian literature was anything but dark and depressing."

"How?" Amy tossed her long, curly hair over her shoulder, crossing her arms over her chest. She knew Ivan was in love with Anna, even if Anna didn't. They were all friends, and he'd confided in her years before about how he felt. This was about more than just convincing Anna that Russian literature was good. This was about winning her best friend's heart.

"I don't know how he plans on doing it other than I'll be reading a lot of authors whose names I can barely pronounce," Anna stated. She turned to her dresser and began tossing underwear into the bag.

Amy walked over to the bag and retrieved the panties. "Uh...no. You're going to be with

Ivan, and you're going to need something way more sexier than these," she stated. She carried the undies back to Anna's dresser and began to go through the lingerie. "Girl, do you not have anything more appropriate for a week with the Russian hunk?"

"Um…I'm not planning on Ivan seeing my underwear," Anna protested as she picked up the offending undergarments and put them back in her bag.

Amy threw her hands up in the air. "That's it. We're going shopping. This is the perfect opportunity for you to find out what your best friend is packing in his tight blue jeans."

"Amy!"

Amy looked at her watch. They had enough time to get to the lingerie store, grab a bite, and finish packing before Ivan showed up to pick up Anna. "I'm trying to get you laid." She tossed Anna her purse. "Whether you want to get laid or not." She grabbed Anna's arm and tugged her out of her apartment. "You can thank me later. Or shoot me if he doesn't live up to your expectations in bed."

"You're assuming we're going to sleep together!" Anna sighed as she fell into step with the other woman.

"You're sleeping together." Amy held up her hand, flagging down a taxi. Shoving Anna into the car, she got in and gave the driver the address to Victoria's Secret in Times Square. "And if you don't, I'm taking you to the hospital myself and having you committed." She grinned. "Cause, let's face it. Ivan is a hunk; you have the hots for him, and it's time for you to just give in to what all of us see right in front of us."

"Which is what?" Anna grumbled.

"You and Ivan Petrov are in love, and it's about time one of you did something about it." Amy chuckled. "You can play his game."

"I don't want to play any games. I just want my time slot back," Anna groused. She watched the people walking on the sidewalks of New York City, going about their lives. She always wondered who they were and what they did for a living. Did they have a family? Were they married? Did they find the love they always wanted, or were they single and carefree? Were they happy? Were they sad? She stopped the thoughts before they could take any deeper hold. Her questioning was starting to sound like one of those Russian novels she found so dark and depressing.

"Besides, you are both consenting adults. What happens in Sleepy Hollow stays in Sleepy Hollow, right?"

Right, indeed. Anna sighed. She knew Amy was right, and she had to decide now before her credit card took a hit with all the sexy clothing Amy was about to make her buy. "I don't want whatever happens between us to ruin our friendship," she finally admitted. She shifted in her seat to look at her friend.

"Might I interject, ladies?" the cabbie asked.

"Please. Tell this girl she needs to give in to her carnal instincts," Amy encouraged.

"If the young man is offering up his home, buying groceries, and wanting to spend time with you, he ain't looking for some one-night stand. He's looking for someone he can form a connection with." The cabbie peered back at them as they sat at the stoplight. "Why enjoy what he's offering up?"

"The light's green," Anna stated, pointing to the front of the car. She sighed in resignation. "Now I'm getting advice from a cabbie."

"Married thirty years. I still woo her every weekend with date night," he claimed proudly.

That made Anna smile. If only she could be so lucky to be wooed like that. But maybe that's what Ivan had planned. Maybe the pilfering of her time slot was a more elaborate ruse to get her alone so that they could finally address the sparks that seemed to fly between them every time they were in the same room together. It made her feel a little better. And Amy was right. She couldn't very go with the plain cotton panties in her dresser, even if she preferred them.

She handed the cabbie a twenty, and as he pulled up to Victoria's Secret, she waited for Amy at the door. "No thongs."

"Oh god, no. You wouldn't catch me dead in a pair of those. My teeth need to be flossed, not my ass," Amy stated in horror. "But go with something a bit sexier." She walked past Anna, pulling the pair of boy cuts from her hand and putting them back on the display. She took her arm and drug her deeper into the store. "Trust me. By the time we're done in here and Ivan sees you in what I have in mind, you will be singing my praises from here to Jersey."

An hour later, Anna emerged with three bags of goodies from Victoria's Secret. She was lucky they were having sales, and her credit card wasn't groaning quite as much as she thought it would. She had everything from sexy bikinis to cheeky panties to bras that cupped her breasts just right while emphasizing her cleavage, which, to be fair, needed as much help as they could get. She had yoga pants to relax in, nighties that were slinky, and even a pair of satin pajamas in case she was too shy to get undressed. A few t-shirts with PINK all over them and some new body spray finished the purchase. They had a quick bite and headed back to her apartment.

"You know, part of me hopes you're right, and part of me doesn't," Anna exclaimed as she finished packing the new clothing in her bag. She looked at Amy. "You sure you don't mind watching Sebastian until I get back?"

"I do not mind watching Sebastian. Cal likes it when he comes to visit. They'll tear up my place from top to bottom, but they do give the best cuddles, and I love falling asleep to purring in stereo. Let's get him in his carrier, and I'll get out of your hair."

It took them a few minutes to wrangle Sebastian into his carrier, but Anna gave him plenty of treats and pets before Amy whisked him away for a long playdate at her house. Anna's stomach was in knots. She knew she had no reason to be nervous, but she was. She looked up as Ivan's car pulled up in front of the apartment building. Picking up her duffle bag, she walked out of the building, ready to face the challenge he had put in front of her.

Chapter Three

Anna had only seen pictures of the house in Sleepy Hollow, and they did not do the home justice. She followed Ivan through it as he showed her the bedroom he thought she would enjoy staying in and then the master bedroom where he would stay. While the house belonged to his parents, they were never there. Instead, they spent their time traveling around the world or toodling across the United States in their RV. Their "mobile home away from home," as Ivan called it. He had commandeered the master bedroom as soon as they took off in the RV the very first time five years earlier and never gave it up. They didn't mind.

"So if you need to work on any lesson plans, you're more than welcome to share my office," he offered, showing her the third bedroom in the house. It was set up with two back-to-back desks with extra monitors and plenty of desk space to work. "I know I haven't finished mine yet, and the morning sun makes this room warm and enjoyable."

Anna looked at the room and felt a pang of jealousy. Her one-bedroom apartment was barely big enough for a dining room table, let alone a dedicated office. "I will be taking you up on that," she stated. She looked at the connection for the extra monitor and smiled. "I'm going to get spoiled like this. I don't have an office at home, and you know I share the one at the university with two other professors." She glanced sideways at him. "Unlike you, who has an office all to yourself."

"You're more than welcome to share mine. I've told you that before," Ivan pointed with a wave of his slender hand. He leaned in the doorway of the room, arms crossed, and simply watched her as she examined the books on the shelf and the movie posters on the wall. He loved old movies, and even though the posters were reprinted, they made him happy.

"Errol Flynn's *The Adventures of Robin Hood*. I love that movie," Anna stated. "And *The King and I*." She pointed to the poster with Yul Brynner. "My mom named me after her."

"Anna in the movie?" He smiled. "And you're a teacher, so that is quite fitting, *dushenka*." He tucked his hands in the pockets of his jeans. "Did you know that he was born in Vladivostok?" He walked over to where Anna was standing, looking at the poster. "He had Buryat blood...Mongol blood. Did you know that?"

Anna shook her head. "No. I always wondered, though, because he looked so natural playing King Mongkut. I would've loved to see him play that part live on stage," she replied. Together, they left the room and headed downstairs.

"Agreed. But we will have to be happy with the movie instead, which I own." He walked across the hardwood floor, through the open-concept living room, and towards the kitchen. "We should watch it one night." He opened the refrigerator and pulled out a bottle of red wine. He waited until she sat at the bar across from him before pouring her a glass. "Dinner will be ready in a few. I hope you don't mind that I cooked."

Anna took the glass he handed her. "I don't mind at all. You know I love your cooking." She took the wine glass and wandered into the living room. The room was bathed in the soft glow of a single lamp, its light casting long shadows across the bookshelves that were filled from floor to ceiling with books. The air was thick with the scent of old paper and ink, mingling with the aroma of Russian Meatball Soup. "When did you have time to make the soup?" she asked, her eyes wandering along the spines of the books on the shelves.

Ivan shrugged. "I started it this morning and pretty much had it ready before I came to pick you up. I'm mostly warming it up and adding the final touches." The living room, with its soft leather sofa and armchair, was a fitting atmosphere for the evening he had planned. He saw Anna sit in the leather armchair, her eyes still wandering over the spines of the books surrounding her, each one a promise of untold stories. He walked over to the bookshelf, wine glass in hand, and let the fingers of his free hand trail over the titles as if choosing the perfect book was a delicate art. He didn't want to start their exploration of Russian romantic literature with something that would chase her away. He paused before pulling out a slender volume, its cover worn and faded. The name embossed on the cover was still clear: Alexander Pushkin. "I think this is a good place to start," Ivan said, his voice low, almost a whisper. He walked over to Anna, holding the book out to her. She took it, feeling the weight of history and passion in her hands.

"Pushkin," Anna murmured, her fingers brushing over the cover. "His words are... intoxicating."

"Yes," Ivan agreed, his eyes darkening with something unspoken. He sipped his wine and motioned to the book with the hand holding the glass, "Pushkin understood the depths of desire, the hunger beneath the surface of civility. Let me show you." He took the book back from her, opening it to a page he had already marked. Clearing his throat, he began to read, his voice rich and velvety, each word laced with seduction.

> *"I recollect that wonderous meeting.*
> *That instant, I encountered you.*

When, like an apparition fleeting,
Like beauty's spirit, past you flew.

Long since, when hopeless grief distressed me,
When noise and turmoil vexed, it seemed
Your voice still tenderly caressed me,
Your dear face sought me as I dreamed."

Ivan's eyes flicked up to meet Anna's as he continued, his voice dropping even lower as though he were sharing a secret. He settled on the coffee table in front of her, setting his glass of wine aside and laying his now free hand on her knee.

"Years passed; their stormy gusts confounded
And swept away old dreams apace.
I had forgotten how you sounded,

Forgot the heaven of your face.

In exiled gloom and isolation
My quiet days meandered on,
The thrill of awe and inspiration,
And life, and tears, and love, were gone.

My soul awoke from inanition,
And I encountered you anew,
And like a fleeting apparition,
Like beauty's spirit, past you flew."

Anna felt a shiver run down her spine, the words seeping into her, awakening something deep and primal. She couldn't tear her gaze away from Ivan, his hazel eyes burning into hers as he read. His voice was rich and seductive, and if this was how he read passages in his class, it was no wonder he had male and female students scrambling to take his class. However, she had a sneaky suspicion that this was all for her and her alone. She took a sip of her wine, letting it linger on her tongue for a moment as she stared at him.

Ivan stood up and walked around the back of the chair. He leaned in closer, his breath warm against her ear as he whispered the final lines.

"My pulses bound in exultation,
And in my heart once more unfold
The sense of awe and inspiration,
The life, the tears, the love of old."

The silence that followed was heavy with unspoken desires. Anna's breath hitched as she felt the intensity of the moment, the line between literature and reality blurring. She couldn't move as she let the implications of the poem sink in. She could feel his breath warm on her cheek until he finally moved. She slowly turned to look at him. Was this how he felt about her?

"Pushkin wrote of love," Ivan said softly, closing the book and standing up, "but he also understood the power of desire, the way it can consume us if we let it." He returned the thin book to its place on the bookshelf before walking into the kitchen and stirring the pot of soup.

Anna's pulse quickened, her thoughts a whirlwind of emotions she had long kept hidden. She followed him, grabbing the bottle of wine and refilling her glass. "And what if we do let it?" she asked, her voice barely audible. There were butterflies in her stomach, and she had never heard a poem more beautiful or more seductive than the one he had just read to her.

Ivan's hand reached out, gently brushing a strand of hair behind her ear. "Then we explore it together, *dushenka*," he replied, his eyes never leaving hers. "Through Pushkin, and others like him, we can give in to those desires, in the safety of words... or perhaps, beyond them." He cupped her cheek for a moment, his palm wam, before picking up the ladle and dishing out their soup.

Anna nodded, the decision already made in her mind. The poem was only the beginning, a gateway to something much deeper, much more intimate. And with Ivan as her guide, she was ready to explore it all.

Chapter Four

Dinner had been a quiet affair full of glances over wine glasses and the promise of things that were long in coming. Ivan had put on some soft music, Tchaikovsky, from what Anna could tell. It wasn't a piece she knew, but then, *The Nutcracker* was pretty much the only piece of music by the Russian composer she was familiar with. She was tired and restless, and the way Ivan looked at her made her cheeks flush. She wasn't used to him looking at her that way.

Or maybe she was, and she just stopped noticing it because she didn't want to admit that she felt the same way about him.

She looked up as the clock on the mantlepiece struck one. She didn't realize that they had been talking for that long. The dim light of a single candle flickered on the coffee table between them, casting dancing shadows across the shelves of books that took up the corner of the living room. Outside, everything was quiet, the world oblivious to the intense conversation unfolding inside.

Ivan sat across from Anna on the couch. He held a worn copy of *Lolita* in his fingers. The book's cover was creased, and its pages slightly yellowed, evidence of the many hands it had passed through before reaching theirs. But it was not just any book—it was Vladimir Nabokov's most infamous work, a novel that had sparked outrage and fascination in equal measure. It was banned from many libraries and reading lists, but regardless of the material, it was still a significant literary work.

Anna's fingers traced the arm of the chair she sat in absentmindedly as she spoke, her voice contemplative. "It's disturbing, isn't it? The way Humbert Humbert manipulates everything, including the reader's sympathies."

Ivan leaned back in his chair, his eyes sharp and thoughtful. He watched her finger trace the scratches in the worn leather. "Nabokov was a master of language, that's for sure," he replied. "And he made us complicit in the story, forcing us to see through Humbert's eyes, even as we recoiled and condemned his actions."

"It draws the reader in, and you can't help but finish reading it, even with all the depravity. It's like watching a train wreck. You can't pull your eyes away from it." Anna nodded, her mind racing with the complexity of the characters. "The way Humbert rationalizes his obsession with Lolita, his justifications... It's terrifying and yet so... compelling. You can't help but be drawn into his twisted world. You can't help but feel something as you read it."

Ivan reached for the book, flipping it open to a passage he had underlined. He cleared his throat, his voice taking on a more measured tone as he read:

> *"A normal man given a group photograph of school girls or Girl Scouts and asked to point out the comeliest one will not necessarily choose the nymphet among them. You have to be an artist and a madman, a creature of infinite*

melancholy, with a bubble of hot poison in your loins and a super-voluptuous fl a m e p e r m a n e n t l y aglow in your subtle spine (oh, bow, you have to cringe and hide!), in order to discern at once, by ineffable signs—the slightly feline outline of a cheekbone, the slenderness of a downy limb, and other indices which despair and shame and tears of—t e n d e r n e s s

> *forbid me to tabulate—the little deafly demon among the w h o l e s o m e children; she stands unrecognized by them and unconscious herself of her fantastic power."*

He paused, letting the words hang in the air, heavy with meaning.

Anna's breath caught as she absorbed the sheer intensity of the prose. Nabokov's language was like a siren's song, beautiful and dangerous, pulling them deeper into the story's dark heart. "How can something so wrong be written so beautifully?" Anna whispered, almost to herself. Her eyes met Ivan's, and she saw the same fire reflected there—a shared understanding of the novel's allure.

"That's the genius of Nabokov," Ivan said, his voice low and velvety. "He challenges our morals, our comfort zones, making us question where the line between art and morality truly lies." He looked further down the pages. "Like this description here:"

> "Here are two of King Akhenaten and Queen Nefertiti's pre-nubile Nile daughters (that royal couple had a litter of six), wearing nothing but many necklaces of bright beads, relaxed on cushions,

intact after three thousand years, with their soft brown puppy bodies, cropped hair and long ebony eyes."

Nabokov's description of the Nile daughters painted an exquisite picture in her mind. She could see them the way he described them in her mind's eye. Anna felt a thrill of excitement, a forbidden curiosity sparked by their discussion. "It's like a dance on the edge of a knife," she mused. "The danger of succumbing to his prose, of allowing yourself to be excited by it, makes the whole tale... intoxicating."

Ivan leaned forward, his gaze intense. "Perhaps that's why we're so drawn to it," he said, his voice barely above a whisper. "It awakens something primal, something we often keep buried. It goes against the societal norms because it is a story about a man who is a pedophile written with such beauty, with such passion that we want to be drawn in while knowing it's not right."

Anna's heart raced, and the room suddenly felt much smaller and more intimate. The intellectual stimulation of their conversation had bled into something more personal, more visceral. She could feel the electricity in the air, the unspoken desires that Nabokov's words had stirred within them. "The way he describes Lolita," Anna continued, her voice softening, "not just as a girl, but as an idea, a concept of nymphet..."

"She could be any girl coming into puberty. Any girl in that awkward stage between child and teenager."

Anna bit her lower lip for a moment. "It's unsettling, yet it speaks to something deeper about the nature of desire, doesn't it?"

Ivan nodded slowly, his eyes never leaving hers. "It's not just about the object of that desire, but about what it represents—the forbidden, the unattainable, the dangerous." He stood up and walked into the kitchen. He picked up the wine bottle and carried it back into the living room. He offered her the first glass, but she held up her hand, stopping him from refilling her glass. He poured the rest of the bottle into his glass, setting the empty on the coffee table next to the candle. He sat back down.

Anna felt a shiver of anticipation. The conversation had taken on a life of its own, moving beyond the pages of the book to something far more personal. "Do you think," she began hesitantly, "that Nabokov wanted us to see a reflection of our own desires in Humbert's obsession? To confront the parts of ourselves, we'd rather ignore?"

Ivan smiled, a knowing glint in his eyes. "Perhaps," he said, his voice a mere murmur. "Or perhaps, *dushenka*, he wanted us to understand that desire, no matter how twisted, is a part of what makes us human." Anna had no idea how long he had wanted to sit with her and talk about literature and how long he wanted to delve into these topics with her. Just her. They never had the chance to do it during college and in the years they spent teaching others. They sat in silence for a moment, the weight of their words settling over them. Ivan reached out, his hand hovering just above Anna's. She looked up at him, her breath catching as she saw the intensity in his gaze. He entwined his fingers with hers, leaning forward to brush his lips over her knuckles. "Like I stated earlier when we were reading Pushkin, desire," he repeated, his voice a caress, "can consume us if we let it."

Anna's pulse quickened, the boundary between their discussion and their own emotions dissolving. His lips were soft over her knuckles, his breath warm. "Show me," she whispered before she lost her nerve. Her heart was racing in her chest. This had gone beyond Ivan, proving to her that Russian literature was sensual and romantic. This was now the culmination of feelings they had danced around for years.

Ivan's lips brushed against hers, sending a jolt of electricity through her. "Are you sure?" he said softly, "because I don't want to do anything you don't want to, *dushenka*. I am patient. I've waited this long to be with you,"

Anna leaned forward, kissing him. She had wanted to do that for a long time, and the brushing of his lips against hers was enough encouragement for her to make the first move. She ended the kiss and leaned back, her breath coming quickly. "I want you," she whispered, leaning her forehead against his. "I don't know why I haven't told you before, but I want you, Ivan."

Her simple words, "I want you," were enough to prompt Ivan into action. He kissed her hungrily, wrapping both arms around her waist and standing up. He felt her wrap her legs around his waist, her fingers in his hair as he carried her upstairs to his bedroom. He set her on her feet, his hands finding the edge of the t-shirt she was wearing and pulling it over her head. He pulled his shirt off as well, his hand finding her soft breasts as his mouth returned to hers. She was soft and warm, and she was everything he had been imagining.

Anna had invaded his dreams. Her smile was the last thing that would fade from his mind, like the Cheshire Cat, when he woke up in the middle of the night, sweating, aroused, and needing her touch. He let his mouth drift down her neck, swirling his tongue in the hollow of her collarbone, tasting her flesh as his hands gently kneaded her breasts. He let one thumb flick over her nipple, teasing it into a tight peak before kneeling before her to take it in his mouth. He scraped his teeth over the taught peak, making her moan in pleasure. Her hands held his head against her, her fists pulling his hair without meaning to but heightening his arousal even more.

Ann couldn't figure out which end was up. The air between them was charged with lightning like a summer storm stalling overhead and breaking over them. Ivan's hands and mouth were a balm to her fevered skin, and she could only hold on to his shoulders as he moved from one breast to the other, his hand replacing his mouth. She could feel every touch, every squeeze, every spot that he was slowly branding as his own. She gazed down at him, watching him. His eyes met hers, and he released her breast to stand back up and kiss her hungrily.

Ivan took her hand and guided it to the front of his jeans. He held it there. "That's what you do to me," he whispered, his voice low and husky. When she rubbed her hand along his length, he moaned in pleasure. He gathered her long hair in his left hand, backing her up against the bed as he kissed her, his free hand sliding between them to palm her through the sweatpants she was wearing. There was nothing wrong with a little innocent teasing to ratchet up the need to come together. Plus, he couldn't get enough of her sweet mouth.

Anna wasn't completely innocent when it came to sex. The one time she had it, it was less than spectacular. She couldn't understand what the fuss was, why her friends enjoyed it so much. *Wait until you meet the right guy*, Amy had told her. *He will set your world on fire, and you will wonder if you will ever stop burning.* Ivan had definitely set her on fire. His hand between her legs, rubbing gentle circles along her flesh combined with the roughness of her lace panties and the pants, was driving her insane. Heat pooled at the site of his fingers, and she couldn't stop the soft shudders that ran through her body.

Ivan could tell she was fighting to keep in control, but the way her hand moved along him spoke volumes. He stopped his slow torment, picking her up at the waist and setting her down on the bed. As he backed away, he peeled off her pants and the lace panties, letting them drop to the floor. He shed his own pants, kissing the inside of her thighs before settling next to her on the bed, one leg draped over hers. He ran his hand up her right leg, coaxing her to part them. He slowly let his fingers go back to teasing her, watching as she arched her back on the bed. He traced slow circles over her pearl, taking his time. He lowered his mouth to the breast that was enticing him, lapping at her hardened nipple.

Anna wasn't sure how much she could handle. The pressure was building, and Ivan was playing her body expertly as if she were a fine instrument. When the heat of her release was more than she could bear, she cried out. She felt him slide his fingers into her, making her shudder even more as he kept the heat burning inside of her. He found her mouth, and she wrapped her arms around his neck, holding on to him like he was the only thing left floating in an ocean of sensation and need.

Ivan brought her to her peak again and then one more time before settling back on the bed. He coaxed her to straddle him. He eased himself inside her tight sheath and moaned, stilling her hips with his hands for a moment. "Not yet, *dushenka*," he purred, his Russian accent very noticeable with his arousal. "Come here."

Anna leaned down, kissing him, her tongue dancing with his, his body buried in hers. She could hear the crickets and other night animals singing from the open bedroom windows, the perfect soundtrack to their lovemaking. She couldn't stay still any longer, and she slowly sat up, rocking her hips over his length.

She was the most exquisite woman Ivan had ever seen. She looked like a siren above him, rising from the waves to save him before his ship could crash down on the rocks. He linked his hands with hers, letting her set the pace. She smiled down at him, and it was like a punch in the gut, almost undoing him right then and there. He had wanted her from the day they first met when she said hello and welcomed him into her life. He knew then he had wanted to make Anna his, and she was worth the wait.

Ivan sat up, kissing her as she quickened her pace. He held her tightly to him, meeting her body with his, every thrust closer to the release they both needed. He kissed her neck as she leaned back against his arms, her soft cries of pleasure spurring him on. His mouth found one breast, suckling it gently. It made her rhythm falter, and he took control. He thrust up into her, his hands sliding to grip her firm behind.

All Anna could do was hold on as he thrust, taking them both higher than they had ever been before. She was on fire, and within moments, it washed over her again and again. She cried out as she rode wave after wave of pleasure, Ivan's own release coming soon after as her body milked his. He buried his face in the crook of her neck, both trembling with the intensity of their lovemaking.

He laid back down on the bed, bringing Anna with him, her body a comfortable weight on his. He let his breathing come back to normal, kissing her hair, her shoulder, and her forehead. She looked up at him, her eyes heavy with contentment, and kissed him before lying down on the bed next to him. He rolled to face her, finding her hand and entwining their fingers. The heaviness of sleep fell on them, and Anna curled against him, wrapping his arm around her, their hands still clasped.

Chapter Five

Anna walked into the Sleepy Coffee, Too coffee shop and stopped dead in her tracks. Not only Amy was there, but Stephanie and Andre were also there. They were part of the bigger "tribe" she and Ivan had built during their time in college. She was surprised to see Stephanie and Andre, and before their appearance in the shop could completely register in her mind, she found herself engulfed in one of Andre's signature bear hugs. Anna laughed. "Put me down, you big oaf!" she teased, playfully smacking his arms. She turned to Stephanie and hugged her before giving

Amy a hug as well. "You didn't tell me they were tagging along," she said as she sat in the empty chair at the table.

"Well, I kinda found them hitchhiking on the side of the road. I took pity on them," Amy quipped, sipping her hot coffee.

"We were in town and called Amy to get together. She said she was coming up here to see you." Andre leaned in towards Anna, dropping his voice a bit. "What's this? We're hearing that you're up here alone with Ivan?" He winked at her, grinning.

Anna shook her head. "It's not what you think. Ivan was being a turd, and I'm attempting to win a bet."

"Uh-huh," Amy grunted behind her coffee cup.

Stephanie reached out to the waitress as she brought her coffee over. "C'mon, Anna. We all know you like Ivan, and he likes you. This isn't over winning a bet."

"Can I get you something?" the waitress asked Anna.

Anna knew she was going to have a hard time with these three, and she sighed. "Yes, let me have a large chai latte and a slice of pecan pie." She waited until the waitress walked away to put in her order. She opened her mouth to speak when another member of the staff stopped at their table with Andre's drink. "And it is over winning a bet," she insisted when the waiter walked away. "Ivan got the director to swap two of our classes, and he snagged a time slot I've had since I started teaching there to accommodate a few students. We got into the discussion over whether or not Russian literature was sensual and romantic and erotic, and he bet me that if he couldn't prove to me it was before we started teaching this semester, he'd give me my slot back."

They all stared at her. "You're staying with Ivan at the family home by yourself to win a bet against a guy who lives and breathes Russian literature and all that goes with it." He started laughing. "And it's not what we think?" He reached out to take her hand. "Anna, babe, it's exactly what we think."

"That's what I said," Amy quipped.

Stephanie grinned, setting her coffee down and wrapping her hands around the mug. "Anna, honey, you're squirming in your seat. Your face is flushing just at his name." She nudged Andre. "Ten dollars says he's already been in her knickers."

"You're on," Andre stated, putting the ten dollars on the table.

"Hey!" Anna exclaimed, trying not to laugh. She forgot how well Andre and Stephanie could read her. Apparently, she had no poker face whatsoever. She hung her head with a frustrated sigh. "Give her the ten bucks," she said quietly.

"Shit, I should've got in on this," Amy laughed as Andre handed Stephanie the money. "Well? Spill the tea, woman. We've all been waiting for you two to hook up. What was it? Pushkin push you over the edge? Nabokov get him to show you his naboknob?"

Anna spit out her coffee at Amy's words. "Oh my god, Amy!" she laughed. I cannot believe you just said that." She took the napkin Stephanie offered and wiped the coffee off her shirt. "For your information, we got into a very interesting conversation about romantic prose, and one thing led to another in the heat of the moment."

"So...was he any good?" Amy continued innocently.

"Is he packing?" Stephanie asked.

"I don't need to know that," Andre stated, leaning one arm on the back of his chair.

"The sex was great. I'm not telling you if he's packing, and that's all I'm going to say on the matter,"

"What matter?" Ivan asked as he stepped up behind Anna. He had seen his friends in the coffee shop as he was walking past on his way to the post office, and he knew Anna was meeting Amy for coffee. He didn't expect to see the others. He had put his fingers to his lips when he walked in, the others not acknowledging him as he listened to the conversation. He laid his hands on Anna's shoulders and leaned down to kiss her cheek before breathing in her scent. "Can I join you, *dushenka*? I would love to know why your cheeks are so warm," he breathed in her ear. He nipped at her ear lobe before standing up and grabbing another chair. "Americano, please," he called to the waitress as she started towards them.

Anna shivered at the lower purr in her ear and lifted her coffee to her lips. She couldn't look at her friends right away. "How much did you hear?" she asked Ivan.

Ivan chuckled. "All of it." He took her hand in his and raised it to his lips with a grin. Her face went redder, and they all chuckled. "Face it, they've known all along how we feel about each other, even if we still are working through it."

"Working through it? Man, you done worked it already," Andre stated, slapping his hand on the table. He winked at Anna. "Ain't nothing to be embarrassed about. We're just happy to see this finally happening." He clapped Ivan on the shoulder. "So, what else has been going on in New York City? How's your family doing?"

Anna listened to the conversation, turned to sports and extracurricular activities that didn't involve her love life, and slowly relaxed. It was good to be with them, for all of them to be together like this. She gazed at Ivan, who still held her hand, and smiled.

Chapter Six

A few days after having coffee with their friends, Ivan and Anna spent the afternoon walking through Sleepy Hollow, taking in the stores and the total Halloween vibe the village seemed to have all year round. They stopped at the two bookstores in town and picked up a few things just for fun before heading back to the house and having a quiet dinner. Anna curled up in the leather armchair in the master bedroom after dinner with a cup of tea and the new journal she purchased. A book by a local author sat to her right on the arm of the chair, but she planned to save that for when they got back to the city. She gazed up at Ivan as he wandered the room for a moment, speaking in Russian to his parents, who had called to see how he was doing. He sank to the Persian rug beneath his feet, patting it and inviting her to join him. She set aside her journal and moved her cup of tea to the small table below the window before settling before him.

The room had become their sanctuary, the floor littered with books open and closed, each one a doorway to a world where passion, love, and desire reigned supreme. She felt like he had hauled half of the bookcase upstairs, and the smell of leather-bound books permeated the air, mingling with the cool breeze that blew into the room. They had spent countless hours here, reading, discussing, and exploring the depths of Russian literature. But tonight, something was different. There was electricity in the air, a tension that had been slowly building with every page turned, every line read aloud. It was as if the words themselves had come alive, wrapping around them, pulling them closer together.

Ivan hung up the phone and tucked it in the pocket of his jeans. "No, where were we?" He sat down across from Anna, a copy of *Dark Avenues* by Ivan Bunin in his hands, his fingers brushing the worn cover with reverence. He opened it to a passage that had struck him deeply, one he knew would resonate with Anna as well. "Listen to this," he said, his voice a low, resonant murmur, heavy with the weight of the words he was about to share. "This is from "Galya Ganskaya." It starts with the the artist kissing Glaya in *"the warm pink body of the beginning of the thigh, then again in the half-open mouth"*."

"Well, that's one way of describing a woman's pussy," Anna chuckled. She bit her lower lip, intrigued with the way Ivan would read these passages to her.

He continues, his voice soft and intimate, as though sharing a secret meant only for them.

"In one minute, I threw off her silk white blouse, and, you know, my eyes just darkened at the sight of her pinkish body with a tan on her shiny shoulders and the milkiness of her corset-lifted breasts with scarlet protruding nipples. When I brutally threw her on the cushions of the sofa, her eyes turned black and widened even more; her lips parted feverishly - as I see all this now,

she was unusually passionate..."

Anna closed her eyes, letting the words seep into her, feeling the way they intertwined with her own thoughts and desires. There was a raw, unfiltered passion in Bunin's writing, a kind of emotional nakedness that mirrored what she and Ivan were slowly uncovering in each other. She listened as he read more, mesmerized by the sultriness in his voice. Yes, some of the literature was rough and dark and long, but everything Ivan had shared with her, everything that they explored so far, was romantic and, in the case of Bunin, erotic. "It's like he's describing us," Anna whispered, her voice trembling with the realization. "This... connection we have, it's more than just words on a page. It's something... primal."

Ivan's gaze never left her as he placed the book aside, leaning closer, his presence almost overwhelming in its intensity. "Yes," he agreed. "Bunin knew how to capture the essence of passion, of that moment when two people truly see each other when everything else fades away."

Anna opened her eyes, meeting his, and in that instant, the world outside the study ceased to exist. They were no longer just reading the stories—they were living them, breathing them in, allowing them to shape their own narrative. "Ivan," Anna murmured, her voice thick with emotion. "Do you ever feel like we're not just exploring these books, but... each other? As every word we read brings us closer, makes us more... vulnerable?"

Ivan reached out, his hand gently caressing her cheek. "I think that's exactly what's happening," he replied, his touch sending a shiver down her spine. "We're stripping away the layers, just like Bunin's characters. We're letting the words guide us, letting them awaken parts of ourselves we might have kept hidden."

He kissed her slowly, his tongue tasing the tea on hers, the sweetness of the honey she used. "I think we are finding something between us that transcends the stories we're exploring. That transcends our friendship even." Anna's breath hitched as Ivan's fingers traced a path from her cheek down to her collarbone, his touch light and teasing but full of intent. She could feel the heat rising between them, the boundary between their literary explorations and their desires dissolving completely. "Like this," Ivan murmured, leaning in until his lips were just a breath away from hers. "This is where the stories come alive and become our story."

Anna closed the distance between them, her lips meeting his in a kiss that was both tender and fierce, filled with all the passion that had been simmering beneath the surface. It was as though Bunin's words had unlocked something within them, something they could no longer keep at bay. Their kiss deepened, becoming more urgent as their hands roamed freely, exploring each other with a familiarity born of both physical and emotional intimacy. The room seemed to shrink around them, the outside world fading into insignificance as they became lost in each other.

He pushed her down to the floor, his hands finding her warm skin beneath her shirt. He cupped her breasts before pulling back slightly, his breath warm against her lips. "This," he said, his voice thick with emotion, "this is what Bunin was writing about. That raw, unfiltered connection, where nothing else matters."

Anna's eyes fluttered open, meeting his gaze. His eyes were filled with a mixture of desire and something deeper—something that went beyond the physical. "I feel it too," she whispered, her voice trembling with the intensity of her feelings. "It's like we're creating our own *Dark Avenue*, where every touch, every word, is a step deeper into... us."

Ivan smiled a slow, sensual smile that made her heart skip a beat. "Then let's keep walking down this path," he whispered, his lips brushing against hers as he spoke. "Let's see where it leads us."

And with that, they let go of all hesitation, all fear, and gave themselves fully to the moment. Even their lovemaking after reading Nabokov wasn't as intense, as raw, as the connection they were feeling now. Their connection had become something more—a living, breathing thing that pulsed with every heartbeat, every touch, every whispered word.

Chapter Seven

They didn't leave the house for two days as a summer storm raged through the Hudson Valley. The electricity was out, and Ivan had managed to find every candle he could to keep the downstairs lit. They had enjoyed a light supper of buckwheat blinis with goat cheese and herring, Okroshka – a Russian cold soup – and Walnut Rugelach Ivan had made from his grandmother's recipe the day before. Anna sat curled up on the couch while Ivan wandered the bookshelves, looking for a very particular volume. He was humming himself, and Anna smiled as she watched him. This was a side of her best friend that she had come to love more than she realized she would. The side that wanted to do nothing more than take care of her and show her his culture, his homeland, beyond the politics. Her anticipation was building as she waited for him to choose the work that would guide their journey tonight.

At last, Ivan pulled a book from the shelf, a small smile playing on his lips as he turned to face Anna. "I think this will do," he said, his voice a deep, resonant purr that sent a shiver down her spine. He held up the book for her to see—*Doctor Zhivago* by Boris Pasternak.

Anna's eyes lit up with recognition, her pulse quickening at the sight of the book. "Zhivago," she whispered, her voice filled with reverence. "Such a beautiful yet sad story."

"Exactly," Ivan replied, his eyes darkening with intent. "One filled with passion and desire and the fact that a choice needed to be made. We'll use his words as our guide, letting them lead us to the choices we make tonight."

He approached her slowly, his presence commanding and magnetic, as though he were a character stepping out from the pages of the very book he held. Anna felt her breath catch in her throat as he knelt before her, his gaze never leaving hers. He opened the book to a marked page, the sound of the turning pages filling the silence between them. He asked her to wear something provocative, and she pulled out the slinky negligee Amy had convinced her to purchase. Ivan began to read aloud, his voice rich and velvety, drawing her into the world of Tolstoy's characters.

> *"...This frail, thin girl is charged, like electricity, to the limit, with all conceivable femininity in the*

world. If you come close to her or touch her with one finger, a spark will illuminate the room and will either kill you on the spot or electrify you for life with her magnetically inductive, whining proclivity and sadness."

The words were heavy with meaning, their intensity palpable. Anna's heart raced as she listened to the description of Lara's beauty. Every woman would hope to be described like that. She could feel the power of the literature coursing through her, heightening her senses, making her acutely aware of every breath, every movement, every look they shared.

As Ivan continued to read, he reached out, his hand gently caressing her leg, the touch as light as a whisper. The simple act of contact sent a wave of heat through her, the anticipation growing with every passing second. Ivan's voice was hypnotic, each word weaving a spell around them, binding them together in a shared experience that transcended the physical. He appreciated the negligee she was wearing, the satin outlining her breasts, the small panties peaking from the hem, his fingertips so close to her heat.

> *"She could never have imagined that he danced so well. What clever hands he has, how confidently he held her by the*

waist! But she won't let anyone else kiss her like that. She could have never imagined that so much shamelessness could be concentrated in other people's lips when they were pressed against your own for so long."

"The power of words," Ivan murmured as he closed the book, his hand still resting on her leg, "is that they can create worlds—worlds that we can step into, that we can make our own. Tonight, let's step into this one together."

Anna felt a thrill of excitement at his words, her body responding to the promise they held. She reached out, placing her hand over his, guiding it higher up her thigh. "Take me there," she whispered, her voice trembling with desire. "Show me how deep this world goes."

Ivan's smile was slow and seductive as he leaned in closer, his breath warm against her ear. "I'll take you wherever you want to go," he promised, his voice a low growl that sent a shiver through her. "Tonight, we'll create our own story—one that's written not with ink and paper but with touch and sensation."

He stood, pulling her up with him, his hand sliding around her waist to draw her against him. Anna could feel the hard lines of his body through his clothes, the heat of him seeping into her, igniting a fire that had been smoldering since they first began their literary explorations together. With a swift, decisive movement, Ivan lifted her and carried her to the low bar counter. The marble was cool against her skin as he leaned over her, his eyes burning with intensity. He was no longer just Ivan—he had become a character in their own story, the charismatic guide who would lead her through the twists and turns of their desires.

Anna felt herself surrendering entirely to the moment, to the story they were creating together. She reached up, threading her fingers through his hair, pulling him down for a kiss that was both fierce and tender, filled with the passion that had been building between them for so long.

Their kiss deepened, becoming more urgent as Ivan's hands roamed over her body, exploring, claiming. Every touch was deliberate, every movement calculated to draw out her pleasure, to bring her closer to the edge. The room around them faded into the background, the books on the shelves bearing silent witness to their exploration. As they lost themselves in each other, the words they had read and the stories they had shared became the fuel for their desire, driving them to new heights of passion. Ivan's knowledge of Russian literature had always been his strength, but tonight, it was his knowledge of Anna—of her desires, her fantasies—that guided their journey.

Chapter Eight

Ivan was definitely convincing Anna that Russian literature was romantic, so much so that she asked him to do something different. She wanted to bring some of the characters to life. "You want to roleplay," Ivan asked, making sure he understood exactly what she was asking for.

"Yes. I want to bring some of these characters to life."

Ivan raised an eyebrow at her as he slid the eggs he had been cooking for breakfast onto the plate and then handed it to her. "Which characters, *dushenka*, do you want to bring to life?"

Anna took the plate he handed her and reached for the butter. She smiled a little. "Anna and Count Vronsky."

Ivan raised an eyebrow. "*Anna Karenina*," he murmured, his voice a deep rumble that sent a shiver down her spine. "A woman torn between duty and desire, living on the edge of a precipice." He cracked another egg into the pan, watching her as she ate. "All right. I'm game. Do you want to dress in costume?"

"Well, not period costumes, but something." She shrugged, eating her breakfast. She took a bite of her toast, her eyes challenging him.

Ivan nodded. "Find a dress. And then we will meet here and bring Anna and Count Vronsky alive."

Anna found a dress that would work at the local thrift store. The master bedroom was thick with anticipation, the kind that hung the space between them, electric and charged. Neither of them needed a copy of the book. *Anna Karenina* was Anna's favorite Russian book. She knew it by heart, and if there was only one piece of Russian literature that she would agree was romantic from the start, that was it. The role play inspired by Russian literature's complex, passionate figures was a new adventure for them both.

In the center of the room, a single, grand mirror reflected the scene back at them. Ivan stood near the window, his dark eyes intent on Anna as she finished adjusting her costume—a delicate, lace-trimmed dress that harkened back to the opulent world of 19th-century Russia. She caught his gaze in the mirror, a knowing smile playing on her lips.

"Anna Karenina," Ivan murmured, his voice a deep rumble that sent a shiver down her spine. "A woman torn between duty and desire, living on the edge of a precipice." He was dressed in a simply white button down shirt, his sleeves rolled up to the middle of his forearms, and dark slacks. He could've stepped out of the book easily in his simple dress.

Anna turned to face him, fully stepping into her role. "And you," she said, her voice soft but firm, "Count Vronsky—the man who would see her fall if only to catch her in his arms."

Ivan's lips curved into a smile, but his eyes were dark and intense as he crossed the room to her. "A man willing to risk everything for love," he said, lifting a hand to gently brush a strand of hair from her face. "To defy society's rules, to embrace the scandal for the sake of passion." He paused, gazing at her. "Why are you testing my patience? It has its limits."

It took Anna a moment to remember the line, to remember Anna's response. "What do you mean by that?" she asked.

"I must ask what you want of me!"

"What can I want? I can only want you not to abandon me, as you are thinking of doing. But I don't want that. That is secondary. What I want is love, and it is lacking. "

The tension between them crackled like a live wire, each word they spoke drawing them deeper into the characters they had chosen to inhabit. It wasn't just play-acting—each gesture, each glance was imbued with the weight of the emotions they had explored together, the boundaries between their roles and their true selves blurring until they were one and the same.

"Anna," Ivan whispered, "At this moment, there is only us. The world beyond these walls doesn't matter. What do you choose—your duty or your heart?"

Anna's breath hitched, the gravity of his question pulling her into the depths of the character. She knew what she was supposed to say, what Anna Karenina would say—but tonight, she was both Anna the character and Anna the woman standing before Ivan, torn between the roles they played and the raw, undeniable connection between them.

"I choose you," she finally breathed, her voice trembling with the truth of the words. "I choose desire."

With those words, the last of the walls between them crumbled. Ivan's hand slid around her waist, pulling her flush against him, the heat of his body searing through the fabric of her dress. His lips found hers in a kiss that was both tender and fierce, filled with the desperate need of a man who knew he was risking everything.

The kiss deepened, their passion fueled by the tragic love story they were reenacting. But as they moved together, the lines between Ivan and Vronsky, between Anna and Anna Karenina, began to blur. It was as if they were no longer merely playing roles but channeling the very essence of these characters—bringing to life the turbulent emotions that had been simmering beneath the surface of their own relationship.

They stumbled toward the bed, their movements driven by the same intensity that had fueled the ill-fated lovers in Tolstoy's novel. But unlike those tragic figures, Ivan and Anna were not bound by the same constraints. Here, in this room, at this moment, they were free to explore every facet of their desires, unburdened by the expectations of society.

As they collapsed onto the bed, Ivan's hands roamed over her body with a mix of familiarity and newfound urgency, as if discovering her anew through the lens of their chosen characters. "You're mine, Anna," he whispered against her lips, his voice rough with need. "No one else can have you."

Anna responded in kind, her hands tangling in his hair, pulling him closer. "And you're mine, Vronsky," she whispered back, her voice filled with a possessive passion that surprised even her. "No one else matters."

The room seemed to pulse with the energy of their connection, the echo of the characters' desires mingling with their own. Every touch, every kiss, was a step deeper into the world they were creating together—a world where literature and reality intertwined, where they could lose themselves completely in the roles they played. Their clothes were shed, dropping to the floor in a puddle of lace and cotton. Ivan pulled her to him, his mouth devouring every inch of her flesh. His mouth suckled at her breast while his fingers stoked her core until she cried out. He drove deep into her, needing to feel her surround him with her heat. He rolled them on the bed, watching as she sat up, riding him until they both cried out with release. They collapsed in contentment for the moment.

But their play was not done. As the night wore on, the roles began to shift once more.

The intensity of Anna Karenina and Vronsky's doomed love gave way to a darker, more complex narrative. Ivan pulled back from her, leaning on one elbow, his hand lazily tracing circles around her nipple. His gaze locked with her with a sudden, fierce intensity.

"Raskolnikov," he said, his voice barely more than a growl. "A man driven by his own demons, haunted by the consequences of his actions."

Anna's heart raced as she recognized the new role he was adopting, the brooding, tortured protagonist of Dostoevsky's *Crime and Punishment*. She felt a thrill of fear and excitement as she met his gaze, understanding that their game was taking a darker turn.

"And who am I?" she asked, her voice steady despite the adrenaline coursing through her veins.

"Sonya," Ivan replied, his voice softening with a hint of tenderness. "The woman who sees the good in him, who loves him despite his sins."

Anna felt a shiver run down her spine as she stepped into the role, her body responding to the shift in their dynamic. "I see your pain, Raskolnikov," she whispered, her hand gently cupping his cheek. "But I see your humanity, too. Let me help you carry the burden."

Ivan's breath hitched, the vulnerability in her words cutting through the darkness of the character he had assumed. He leaned into her touch, his eyes closing as he allowed himself to be comforted, to let go of the weight he carried—even if only for a moment.

Their embrace was different now, softer, more intimate, as they explored this new facet of their relationship. It was no longer about passion and desire alone; it was about connection, about understanding and accepting each other's flaws, just as Sonya had accepted Raskolnikov's.

They held each other close, the echoes of the characters' stories fading into the background as they returned to themselves, to the deep, unspoken bond that had brought them to this point. The roles they played were a reflection of the complexities of their own relationship, of the love and passion that had been simmering between them from the start. A love and passion that had been years in the making. As the night drew to a close, Ivan and Anna lay together, their bodies intertwined, their minds still reeling from the intensity of their roleplaying. The room was silent now, save for the soft sound of their breathing.

"We've created something beautiful here," Ivan whispered, his voice filled with awe. "Something real, something that goes beyond the pages of any book."

Anna smiled, her heart swelling with the truth of his words. "Yes," she agreed, her voice soft and full of emotion. "We've written our own story, one that's as complex and passionate as any we've read."

Chapter Nine

The weather in Sleepy Hollow had turned cold and damp. It was the perfect day to stay indoors and get some work done. They were coming down to the wire. Classes would start in a few days, and while both Ivan and Anna worked on their lesson plans for the upcoming semester, they needed to finish them and make sure everything was ready. They spent the day in the office upstairs, the strains of Tchaikovsky and other classical composers setting a backdrop for their work. At some point, Ivan had slipped downstairs and made them lunch, bringing Anna a bowl of soup and grilled cheese while she worked.

That was something she adored about Ivan. He was always doing little things like that. A simple bowl of soup and grilled cheese was the perfect lunch for a rainy day, and he never complained about making it. They shared a shower when they got up to start their day, and he insisted on washing her hair and pampering her. He was still old school in some ways, opening doors, pulling out her chair at restaurants, walking on the outside of a sidewalk so that she wouldn't get splashed. She knew there were some women who wouldn't appreciate the simple gestures, but she did. It was common respect and courtesy, and it was refreshing.

The more she thought about it, the more she realized that Ivan had always been that way, even in college. He doted on her, their friendship building over the years into something more. Something they finally decided to act on. He smiled at her as he walked into the living room, handing her a cup of tea. It was chilly enough to light a fire, and the room was cozy, with the fire crackling merrily in the grate.

Ivan stood by the fireplace, his tall frame illuminated by the dancing light. His eyes, dark and intense, gazed at Anna where she sat in the leather armchair. He had asked her to change after dinner, to wear nothing but her sexiest bra and panties and robe to keep her warm until they started exploring another Russian masterpiece. "Anna," Ivan said softly, his voice a low rumble that sent shivers down her spine. "I want to share something with you—something that requires both trust and openness."

Intrigued, Anna's pulse quickened as she felt the intensity of his gaze. She sipped at her tea and watched him expectant. "Okay. What do you want to share?

Ivan sat across from her, leaning forward slightly, his posture both relaxed and commanding. "We've explored many facets of Russian literature together," he began, his voice smooth and controlled. "But there's a layer we've yet to fully delve into—one that involves the interplay of power, control, and surrender. In these texts, dominance and submission are often subtle, woven into the relationships between characters, but they carry a deep psychological and sensual weight."

Anna's heart raced as she listened, the idea both thrilling and slightly daunting. "You mean...like in *The Master and Margarita*," she said, recalling the complex, almost mystical relationship between the characters. "The way Woland, with his overwhelming power, controls and manipulates the others, yet there's an undeniable allure to it—a seduction in his dominance."

"Exactly," Ivan replied, a pleased smile playing on his lips. "There's a certain allure in the dynamics of control and surrender, where trust is the foundation. This can be mirrored in our own interactions—an exploration of literary BDSM if you will. But it must be consensual, respectful of boundaries, and deeply rooted in mutual desire."

Anna's breath caught in her throat as she considered his words. The idea of surrendering to Ivan, of giving up control within a framework of trust, sent a thrill through her that she couldn't quite name. It wasn't just about physical submission; it was about exploring a new level of their relationship, one where vulnerability and strength coexisted.

"How do we begin?" she asked, her voice soft, tinged with both anticipation and a hint of nervousness. She quickly finished her tea and set it on the side table. She leaned her cheek into Ivan's hand when he cupped it before dropping a soft kiss on her lips.

"Take off your robe. You should be warm enough." Ivan stood and moved to a small table near the bookcases where a few carefully chosen items were laid out—a silk blindfold, a pair of leather cuffs, and an old, worn copy of Dostoevsky's *The Idiot*. He picked up the book, its pages yellowed with age, and returned to her, his gaze never leaving her face. "We start with trust," he said, handing her the book. "In literature, as in life, the dynamics of power can be complex, but they can also be beautiful when explored with care. This book, *The Idiot*, explores the vulnerability of Prince Myshkin, a man who, despite his innocence, finds himself at the mercy of those around him. He is both a victim and, in some ways, a master of his fate—his goodness and purity giving him a power that others don't fully understand." He admired the way the red lace bra hugged her breasts, the way the matching panties curved around her shapely behind.

Anna nodded, her fingers tracing the embossed letters on the cover as she absorbed his words. "I trust you, Ivan," she said quietly, the weight of the admission settling between them.

"Good," Ivan replied, his voice gentle yet firm. He set the book aside and took the silk blindfold in his hands, his movements slow and deliberate. "Close your eyes."

Anna obeyed, her heartbeat echoing in her ears as she felt the cool silk brush against her skin. Ivan tied the blindfold in place, his fingers grazing her neck in a touch that was both tender and authoritative. The darkness heightened her other senses—the sound of his breathing, the warmth of the fire, the subtle scent of the leather from the books and the chair she sat in..

"In this space," Ivan murmured, his lips close to her ear, "you are safe. You are free to explore, to feel, to surrender. The power I have is given by you, willingly, and can be taken back at any time."

Anna's breath hitched as she felt his hands gently securing the leather cuffs around her wrists, the sensation both foreign and electrifying. She felt the tug of the restraints as he fastened them to the wooden slats of the lower portion of the leather armchair, her movements now limited, her body attuned to every nuance of his presence. He patted her legs, curled under her, and she shifted, letting them hang over the edge of the chair, her feet dangling an inch from the floor.

"What do you feel, Anna?" Ivan asked, his voice low, almost hypnotic.

"Exposed," she whispered, the word barely audible. "But also...protected. I'm aware of every touch, every breath. It's...intense."

Ivan smiled with a dark, satisfied expression. "That's the beauty of surrendering control," he said softly. "It amplifies everything—your senses, your emotions. But remember, you are always in control of your surrender." He moved behind her, his hands resting on her shoulders, his touch warm on her skin. He leaned in, his breath hot against her ear as he spoke. "The characters in our favorite books often navigate the boundaries of power and vulnerability, of control and surrender. Like Prince Myshkin, you can choose to embrace your vulnerability, to find strength in it." With a slow, deliberate movement, Ivan's hands slid down her arms, taking the straps of her bra with them until they fell loose. His touch was light yet commanding, sending waves of sensation through her body. The tension between them crackled, the room filled with the unspoken promise of what was to come.

As he continued, he whispered passages from *The Idiot* into her ear, his voice weaving the words into a sensual narrative that intertwined with the physical sensations he was creating. Each passage was carefully chosen, emphasizing themes of power, innocence, and the complex interplay of dominance and submission.

> *"There is something at the bottom of every new human*

thought, every thought of genius, or even every earnest thought that springs up in any brain, which can never be communicated to others, even if one were to write volumes upon volumes about it; but every human being has his secrets, and this is mine." Ivan's voice was a seductive murmur, the words dripping with the weight of hidden desires.

Anna's breathing quickened, the combination of his voice, the restraints, and the darkness pushing her to the edge of her own consciousness, where thoughts and sensations blended into a heady mix of pleasure and anticipation. She inhaled when he reached out to unhook the closure at the front of her bra, exposing her breasts to the warm air of the room. He didn't touch or fondle them, though, teasing her through lack of touch.

Ivan's hands moved to her waist, pulling her slightly forward so that she was more aware of her own body, of the restraints holding her in place. "This is the trust we share, Anna," he whispered, his voice filled with both authority and tenderness. He slid his hands below her, to her behind, and carefully removed her lace panties. "In this space, we explore together—where control and surrender meet, where vulnerability becomes strength." He grasped her ankles and tugged upwards, making her bend her knees and plant her feet on the edges of the armchair, exposing her even more to his hungry eyes. He kissed the inside of her thigh, a soft, lingering touch that sent a shiver through her. The contrast between the gentleness of his kiss and the firm grip of the cuffs was intoxicating, each sensation heightened by the other.

The feeling of the air on her body, the soft crackling of the fire, the erotic position she was in…it all made her heart race. Ivan had stopped speaking. She listened for any sign of him. But everything was still. "Ivan?" she asked softly.

Ivan was slowly and quietly undressing. He knelt before her, licked the tip of his index finger, and slowly stroked it over her slit. She inhaled softly as he slowly stroked her, teasing her, bringing her close to the edge, and stopping for a moment, listening to her breathing speed up and then slow down. He leaned forward and replaced his finger with his tongue, tasting her sweetness, suckling her pearl, as he stroked his own hardened manhood. It was intoxicating to have this power over Anna, and it made him realize that he would do anything for her. She trusted him to guide her into this exploration, and he vowed at that moment never to betray her trust.

He brought her to orgasm, licking up ever drop og her sweet nectar before sliding into her with a soft, gutteral groan, he released her hands from the cuffss and removed the blindfold, pulling her to him in the chair to kiss her as she wrapped her legs around him. He set a steady pace, her hands gripping his shoulders, their tongues dueling for supremacy. They each felt a profound sense of connection—not just to each other, but to themselves. She had discovered new layers of trust, vulnerability, and pleasure, all within the safe confines of their shared exploration, and he discovered how to live within the boundaries they had set forth.

As they lay together afterward, their bodies entwined, Anna felt an overwhelming sense of gratitude for the depth of their relationship. Ivan had guided her through an experience that was both intense and enlightening, one that had brought them closer in ways she hadn't thought possible. She looked up at him, her eyes filled with a mixture of awe and affection. "Thank you," she whispered, her voice thick with emotion. "For trusting me and for helping me discover this part of myself."

Ivan smiled, his hand gently stroking her hair. "Thank you, Anna," he replied softly. "For your trust, your openness. This is just the beginning of our journey—one where we'll continue to explore, to push boundaries, and to find new depths in both our minds and bodies." As they drifted off to sleep, the fire slowly dying down, the room held the lingering energy of their exploration. In this space, the lines between literature and reality had blurred, where power and surrender had merged into a dance of mutual desire and respect.

Chapter Ten

They had returned to the city the Friday before classes started to finish up the last-minute things required of college professors. Anna stood in the kitchen of her cozy apartment while the soft afternoon light filtered through the sheer curtains, casting a warm glow over the living room. It was a comfortable space with a blend of modern elegance and personal touches—framed photographs, a well-stocked bookshelf, a vase of fresh flowers on the coffee table, and Ivan's overnight in the hallway. Anna walked into the living room with the tray of tea and cookies she pulled together, setting them on the coffee table before sitting on the couch, her legs curled under her. She poured Amy a cup of tea and then poured her own, handing Amy the cup. She sat back on the couch, both of them sipping at the fragrant brew.

Amy sipped her own drink, her expression a mix of concern and curiosity. "So," Amy began, setting her cup down and leaning forward slightly, "what's really going on with you and Ivan? You've been… different lately. Happier, yes, but also more reserved. I know something's up." She jerked her thumb to his overnight bag in the hallway. "You two having a sleepover now that we called you out?" she teased lightly.

Anna laughed, biting her lip, her gaze dropping to the steaming cup in her hands. She had been dreading this conversation, knowing that Amy, with her straightforward nature, would demand answers she wasn't sure she was ready to give. But she also knew she couldn't keep everything bottled up.

"It's... complicated," Anna started, her voice hesitant. "Ivan and I...since that day in the coffee shop, we've been exploring some new aspects of our relationship. Things that are... unconventional, I guess you could say."

Amy's eyebrows shot up in surprise. "Define unconventional." It was all she said, sensing that Anna needed to find her own way to explain.

Anna took a deep breath, finally looking up to meet Amy's eyes, and chuckled softly. "We've been exploring power dynamics, dominance, and submission—things that I never really thought about before. Roleplay. It's all consensual, of course, and we've talked about everything. But it's intense, Amy. It's pushed me to confront parts of myself that I didn't even know were there."

Amy's expression shifted to one of surprise and curiosity, but Anna could see the concern lurking in her eyes. "And... how do you feel about it?" Amy asked gently.

"At first, I was scared," Anna admitted. "I didn't know if I could handle it or if it would change how I saw myself. But Ivan has been so patient and careful with me. He's always made sure I feel safe and that I'm in control of what I want to explore. And..." She shook her head, exhaling as she set her teacup on the table. "Wow. It's been liberating, in a way. I feel like I'm discovering a new side of myself, a deeper connection to Ivan. But..."

Amy leaned forward, her voice soft. "But?"

Anna hesitated, the words heavy on her tongue. "But not everyone understands. Some of our friends... okay, Andre... have noticed something different between us, and they disapprove. He came to see me at the coffee shop yesterday, and we were talking, and I told him what was going on. Of all people, I figured Andre would get it. He sees what we're doing as dangerous or just... strange. He made some comments that made me feel uncomfortable and asked me if I was okay and if I needed help. It's like he thinks I'm losing myself or being manipulated. It hurts, Amy. It really hurts."

Amy reached out, placing a comforting hand on Anna's arm. "I'm sorry you're going through this," she said, her voice filled with sympathy. "People can be so quick to judge what they don't understand. And honestly, coming from Andre, I'm not surprised. He's so straight-laced and vanilla." She grinned at her friend. "But Anna, you're one of the strongest people I know. If this is something that makes you happy and helps you grow, then who cares what anyone else thinks?"

Anna gave her a grateful smile. "Thank you. I needed to hear that."

"Did you tell Ivan? I'm surprised he didn't go knock Andre's block off."

"Yeah, and I did. He said the same thing you did. And I wish it were that simple. I love Ivan, and what we have together is something special, something I never imagined I could experience. I went into Pink Pussycat Boutique the other day and picked up a few things that were a bit…well…anyway…every time someone looks at me with pity or disapproval, it's like a stab to the heart. I feel torn between being true to myself and the need to conform to what everyone else expects."

Amy scoffed. "Screw society. Yeah, it's not easy to go against the grain, especially when it comes to something as personal as your relationship. But you deserve to be happy, Anna. You deserve to live your life on your own terms, not based on what others think is right. Besides, what goes on behind closed doors is between you and Ivan."

Anna nodded, feeling a swell of emotion rise within her. "I know you're right. But I don't want to lose the people I care about, either. How do I find that balance, Amy? How do I stay true to myself without alienating everyone around me?"

Amy sighed, her expression thoughtful. "I don't think there's a simple answer to that. You might lose some people along the way, but the ones who truly love you will find a way to understand, even if it takes time. And those who can't accept you for who you are... well, maybe they're not meant to be part of this chapter of your life."

Amy nodded, her expression softening. "I get it. But remember, you're not alone in this. Ivan's with you, and so am I. And I'm sure there are others who'll support you once they see how happy you are and how much this relationship means to you."

Anna smiled, a tear slipping down her cheek as she reached out to hug her friend. "Thank you, Amy. For understanding, for being here. It means more than you know."

Amy hugged her back, her voice warm and reassuring. "I'm always here for you, Anna. No matter what. And for what it's worth, I think you're incredibly brave for following your heart." She reached over to the teapot and refilled their tea cups. "Now. I wanna see what you bought at the Pink Pussycat and see if I can give you some ideas to try with your Russian hunk."

Chapter Eleven

The rain pattered softly against the windows, a rhythmic backdrop to the quiet tension that filled the room. Ivan and Anna sat on the plush sofa in his spacious apartment, a small table with a bottle of wine between them before them. The dim light from a single lamp cast long shadows across the room, adding to the intimacy of the moment. Anna shifted slightly, her fingers tracing the rim of her glass as she searched for the right words. She had always felt safe with Ivan, yet the complexity of their relationship had unearthed insecurities and fears she hadn't anticipated. Finally, she broke the silence.

"Ivan," she began softly, her voice tinged with vulnerability, "I've been thinking a lot about... us. About what we're exploring together. And I can't help but feel conflicted sometimes. I love what we have, but there are moments when I feel this nagging guilt like I'm doing something wrong. I know it's because of how I was raised, the things society drilled into me about what's 'acceptable.' And we work together. The whole 'don't date your coworker' thing, which I know is stupid. But the feeling is hard to shake."

Ivan's eyes softened as he listened, sensing the weight of her words. He set his glass down and reached out, taking her glass and setting it on the table with his own. He gently took her hands in his, raising them to his lips to plant kisses across her knuckle. "I understand, *dushenka*. I feel it, too, more often than I'd like to admit. There's this voice in the back of my mind that questions everything—whether what we're doing is right, whether we're crossing lines that shouldn't be crossed. It's not easy to let go of years of conditioning." He retained possession of her hands. "And I don't want to lose you. You mean the world to me. You have since the day I met you and regret nothing about these last two weeks together."

Anna looked up at him, her eyes filled with a mixture of relief and sadness. "But I don't want to feel this way. I don't want to let fear dictate our relationship. I want to embrace what we have fully, without holding back. But how do we do that when these doubts keep creeping in?"

Ivan sighed, his thumb brushing over her knuckles in a soothing gesture. "It's a journey, *dushenka*. One we have to take together. I think the first step is acknowledging that these feelings are normal and that it's okay to question and have doubts. We've been taught to see our desires as something to be hidden, something to be ashamed of. But they're a part of who we are. And if we want to move forward, we need to accept that, to challenge and replace those old beliefs with our own truths."

Anna nodded, her grip on his hand tightening as she drew strength from his words. She entwined her fingers with his. "You're right. I've been so afraid of what others might think, of what it says about me if I embrace these desires. But when I'm with you, when we're exploring together, I feel more alive, more in tune with myself than ever before. I don't want to lose that because of outdated ideas about what's 'normal.'"

Ivan smiled, a warm, encouraging expression that made her heart flutter. "Neither do I. And that's why we need to communicate, to be open with each other about what we're feeling, what we need. It's not just about what we do together physically—it's about the emotional and psychological aspects, too. We need to establish clear boundaries to ensure that we're both comfortable and safe in every aspect of our relationship."

Anna took a deep breath, her resolve strengthening. "Let's talk about those boundaries then. I want us to be on the same page, to know where each of us stands."

They spent the next hour in deep conversation, discussing their desires, fears, and limits. Ivan shared his thoughts on power dynamics, the importance of trust, and the need for a safe word when they decided to let their bedroom play get crazy, something they could use if either of them felt uncomfortable at any point. Anna spoke about her need for reassurance, for the knowledge that she could always pause or stop if she needed to, without fear of judgment.

Their conversation was raw and honest, filled with moments of vulnerability that brought them closer. They didn't shy away from the difficult topics, from the insecurities that had bubbled to the surface during their exploration. Ivan admitted his fear of losing control, of pushing too far and hurting Anna unintentionally. Anna confessed her anxiety about being seen as weak or unworthy because of her submissive desires. And she admitted that once she was more comfortable, she wanted to see Ivan in handcuffs and show him a night of unbridled pleasure at her hands.

But through it all, they reassured each other, their words weaving a tapestry of trust and mutual respect. By the time they finished, there was a newfound lightness between them, a sense of clarity and understanding that hadn't been there before.

Ivan leaned back against the sofa, pulling Anna into his arms and on his lap. She rested her head on his chest, feeling the steady rise and fall of his breathing. "I'm so glad we talked about this," she murmured, her voice content.

"Me too," Ivan replied, his hand gently stroking her hair. "This is how we grow, *dushenka*, by being open and confronting our fears together. I want you to know that I'm here for you, always. Whatever you need, we'll figure it out."

Anna closed her eyes, allowing herself to fully relax in his embrace. "I believe you. And I want you to know that I'm here for you, too. We'll face whatever comes our way together."

They stayed like that for a long time, wrapped in each other's warmth and the comfort of knowing they were on the same path, committed to navigating their desires and boundaries with care and love.

As the night deepened, the rain outside became a gentle lullaby, lulling them into a peaceful state of acceptance. They had taken a significant step forward, not just in their relationship but in their journey toward self-acceptance and mutual understanding. In that quiet moment, they both realized that their love was strong enough to withstand the challenges ahead, that together, they could rewrite the narrative of what was acceptable, what was possible, and what was beautiful about their unique connection.

"*Dushenka?*" Ivan murmured as they settled under the comforter of his large bed.

"Mmmm?" she replied, snuggling closer to him.

"I love you." He let his fingers trace lines across her shoulder.

"I love you too," she answered, kissing his neck.

"And I want to marry you. Move in with me. Let's plan a summer wedding together."

Anna lifted her head and looked down at him. She smiled in the dim light. "I like that idea. We can set up the spare bedroom as our mutual office, like at your family home."

Ivan shook his head. "No. We move to my family home. I told my parents about my plans to ask you, and they told me to take the house for us."

He reached up to stroke a piece of her hair from her face. "What do you think?"

She leaned forward, kissing him soundly. "Yes, Ivan Petrov. I will marry you, and I will move in with you in Sleepy Hollow, and we will plan the most beautiful summer wedding together."

Ivan rolled her beneath him, kissing her soundly. "Then tomorrow, let's plan our move and put it into action. Monday, in between classes, we can let the movers in to pack us up."

"Agreed." She wrapped her arms around his neck. "There is one thing, though, we still need to discuss?"

"What?" he asked curiously.

She grinned mischievously at him in the dim light of the bedroom. "I still want my time slot back."

"You lost fair and square," Ivan protested, making Anna laugh.

"Did I?" she asked, pulling him down to kiss him again. "Remind me how I lost again," she challenged.

Ivan stared at her before grinning, pulling the covers over his head and wiggling further down her body, making her sigh in contentment.

Chapter Twelve

The flickering candlelight cast a warm, golden hue over the room. They returned to his family home the day before classes started, celebrating a new beginning, a new chapter in their lives. Anna had pretty much packed up her small, one-bedroom apartment, deciding to sell her furniture. Amy bought most of it and was arranging to get someone to the apartment later that week to move it. All her clothing was now hung in the walk-in closet in Ivan's room, and her boxes of knick-knacks, books, and photos were safely tucked away in the spare bedroom upstairs to be sorted out later. Sebastian was sound asleep on the bed in the spare bedroom, settling in immediately in his new home. Tonight, it felt even more intimate, the air charged with anticipation as they prepared to delve deeper into their journey of self-discovery.

Anna stood by the window, gazing out at the city lights that twinkled in the distance. Her reflection in the glass revealed a woman who had transformed over the past two weeks—a woman who had shed layers of fear, guilt, and shame to embrace the fullness of her desires. Ivan approached her, his presence steady and reassuring, the embodiment of the trust and respect they had built together.

"Are you ready?" Ivan asked, his voice a low, soothing rumble.

Anna turned to him, a smile playing on her lips. "More than ever," she replied, feeling a surge of confidence and excitement. They had come so far, navigating the complexities of their relationship with care and understanding, and now, they stood on the precipice of something profound.

Ivan reached for a book on the desk, the cover embossed with Cyrillic script. It was Tolstoy's *Anna Karenina*, a novel that had sparked many discussions between them about passion, love, and the consequences of societal constraints. Tonight, they would use it as a catalyst to push their exploration to new heights.

He opened the book to a marked passage and handed the book to her. "I want to hear you read this one," he said.

Anna began to read aloud, her voice rich with emotion. The words flowed between them, weaving a tapestry of intense longing and desire that resonated deeply within their hearts. As Anna read, Ivan moved closer to her, his hand finding hers, their fingers entwining as the power of the text ignited a fire within them.

> *"He felt now that he was not simply close to her, but that he did not know where he ended and she began."*

She continued to read, her voice dropping to a whisper as she met Ivan's gaze.

> *"It frightened him to realize how much he loved her, but at the same time, it filled him with a sense of elation, of triumph. They were one, bound by something far greater than themselves."*

The passage hung in the air, a perfect reflection of what they had become. Ivan set the book aside and cupped Anna's face in his hands, his touch tender yet filled with the intensity of his emotions. "This is us, Anna. We are more than just two people exploring our desires. We are bound by something powerful, something that defies the norms society tries to impose on us. We are free—free to be who we are, to love as we choose, without shame or guilt."

Anna's breath hitched, her heart swelling with the truth of his words. "I never imagined I could feel this way—so alive, so empowered. With you, I've discovered parts of myself I didn't even know existed, and I've learned to love those parts without fear. I'm not afraid anymore, Ivan. I want to embrace everything we are, everything we can be, with no apologies."

Their lips met in a kiss that was both tender and passionate, a culmination of their journey toward self-acceptance and liberation. As they kissed, they moved toward the center of the room, the intensity between them building with each step. There was no rush, no urgency—only the deep connection that had grown between them, a connection that transcended the physical and touched the very essence of their beings.

In the warmth of their embrace, they began to explore each other with a newfound freedom, their movements guided by the trust and communication they had nurtured. Ivan's hands traced the contours of Anna's body, his touch both commanding and reverent, while Anna responded with equal fervor, her fingers trailing along his skin, her lips whispering words of love and desire.

The bedroom became a sanctuary of passion, their bodies and souls entwined in a dance of mutual discovery. The constraints of society's expectations no longer bound them; instead, they were free to express their deepest fantasies and desires without fear of judgment.

Each caress, each whispered word, was a testament to the empowerment they had found in each other's arms.

As their exploration reached its crescendo, they found themselves at the peak of pleasure and connection, their hearts and bodies aligned in perfect harmony. In that climactic moment, they confronted their innermost desires and fears, allowing themselves to be vulnerable, yet powerful. The intensity of their passion was matched only by the depth of their emotional bond, a bond that had grown stronger with each step of their journey.

When the wave of pleasure finally subsided, they lay entwined on the bed, their breaths mingling in the quiet aftermath. The glow of the candles cast a soft light over their faces, highlighting the contentment and fulfillment that radiated from within.

"I love you, Anna," Ivan whispered, his voice filled with emotion. "And I am so proud of the woman you've become—of the woman you've always been. Together, we've defied the expectations placed on us, and we've emerged stronger for it."

Anna smiled, her heart overflowing with love and gratitude. "I love you too, Ivan. You've shown me that there's no shame in embracing who we are, in finding joy and fulfillment in our desires. We've created something beautiful, something that is ours alone. And I wouldn't trade it for anything."

As they held each other close, they knew that their journey was far from over. There would be new challenges and new desires to explore, but they would face them together with the same trust, respect, and communication that had brought them this far. They had triumphed over their doubts, their fears, and the judgments of others, and in doing so, they had found a love that was both empowering and transformative.

In the quiet of the night, Ivan and Anna drifted into a peaceful sleep, their heart's content in the knowledge that they had found something rare and precious—true freedom and acceptance, not only in each other but in themselves.

CHAPTER THIRTEEN

THE SUN CAST A warm, golden light over the city as Anna and Ivan walked hand in hand down the bustling street. The new semester was about to begin, and the familiar energy of the university campus buzzed around them. Yet, there was something different this time—a sense of calm and confidence that had settled between them, a reflection of the journey they had undertaken together.

They stopped in front of a quaint bookstore, its window display filled with classic Russian literature. Anna smiled, squeezing Ivan's hand as they looked at the titles they had come to know so intimately. These books had been the catalyst for their transformation; the pages they had once turned with curiosity now held a more profound, more personal significance.

"Remember the first time we stood in front of this window? We were college students ourselves," Anna asked, her voice soft with nostalgia.

Ivan chuckled, his eyes crinkling at the corners. "How could I forget, *dushenka*? You were so hesitant to pick up *Lolita*, and now look at us."

Anna laughed, the sound light and free. "Who would have thought that our shared love for these books would lead us here? It's amazing how much has changed."

"And how much we've changed," Ivan added, his tone more serious. He turned to face her, his expression filled with pride and affection. "We've come so far, Anna. We've faced our fears, confronted our insecurities, and embraced parts of ourselves that we used to hide. I'm so proud of us—for everything we've done and everything we've become."

Anna felt a swell of emotion as she met his gaze. She thought back to the moments of doubt, the challenges they had faced, and the deep, soul-searching conversations that had brought them closer together. Their journey had not been easy, but it had been worth every step. They had emerged from the experience stronger, more resilient, and deeply connected.

"I'm proud of us, too," Anna said, her voice steady with conviction. "We didn't let anything stand in our way—not societal expectations, not our own fears. We created something beautiful together, something that's ours and ours alone. And I wouldn't trade it for anything."

Ivan leaned in, pressing a gentle kiss to her forehead. "Neither would I. And I can't wait to see where we go from here."

As they continued their walk, they arrived at the university gates, where students were already milling about, eager for the new semester. The campus felt like a second home, filled with familiar faces and places. But there was something new this time—a sense of belonging, not just to the university, but to each other.

They entered the main building, where they would be teaching their respective classes. The thought of standing in front of a room full of students, sharing their knowledge and passion, filled Anna with excitement. She had always loved teaching, but now, there was an added layer of fulfillment—knowing that she had Ivan by her side, that they were partners in every sense of the word.

As they reached their offices, Ivan turned to her with a mischievous grin. "You know, moving in together might just be the best idea we've had yet. Imagine all the late-night discussions, the impromptu book readings, and maybe a few other things..."

Anna laughed, her cheeks flushing with a mix of excitement and anticipation. "I'm looking forward to it. Our own little haven, filled with books and memories. It sounds perfect."

"It will be," Ivan said, his voice warm with promise. "We'll continue our exploration, push new boundaries, and most importantly, we'll do it together."

Anna felt a sense of peace wash over her. The conflicts and challenges they had faced were behind them now, and in their place was a future filled with possibility. They had built a relationship on trust, communication, and a shared passion for literature, and she knew that whatever lay ahead, they would face it with the same courage and love that had brought them this far.

As they prepared to part ways for their first classes of the day, Ivan pulled Anna into a tight embrace. "I love you, Anna," he whispered into her hair.

"I love you too, Ivan," she replied, her voice filled with emotion. "And I can't wait to see what the future holds for us."

They shared one last kiss before stepping into their respective classrooms, each filled with a renewed sense of purpose and excitement. The city, the university, their new home—everything felt like a fresh start, a new chapter in the story they were writing together.

As Anna stood before her students, ready to dive into the complexities of creative writing, she felt a surge of confidence and joy. She had found her voice, her passion, and her love, all within the pages of the books she now fully understood and adored. And she knew their journey was only just beginning with Ivan by her side.

Resources

Bulgakov, Mikhail, et al. *The Master and Margarita*. Penguin Books Ltd, 2023.

Bunin, Ivan Alekseevich. *Dark Avenues*. Bookking, 1995.

Dostoyevsky, Fyodor, and Constance Garnett. *Crime and Punishment*. Modern Library.

Dostoyevsky, Fyodor, et al. *The Idiot, Novel in Four Parts, by Fyodor Dostoyevsky; Translated from the Russian by Constance Garnett; Illustrated by Boardman Robinson*. Random House, 1935.

Gibian, George, editor. "Aleksandr Pushkin - To..." *The Portable Nineteenth-Century Russian Reader*, Penguin Books, New York, NY, 1993, p. 6.

Nabokov, Vladimir Vladimirovič., et al. *Lolita*. Sanje, 2005.

Pasternak, Boris L. *Dr. Zhivago*. Pantheon, 1958.

Tolstoy, Leo. *Anna Karenina*. Penguin Reader, 2001.

About The Author

Award-winning author Beth A. Freely was born and raised in upstate New York, with a brief and very influential stint living in Great Britain that can be seen in her writing. Today, she calls New Mexico home. When asked how long she has been writing, she'll tell you, "All my life."

In 2003, she published some of her fanfiction online and won awards for her stories. Two years later, she was the 1st Place winner of the 2005 Arche Books Publishing Novel Writing Contest in Women's Fiction with her novel *Behind the Eyes of Dorian Gray*. In 2022, she took home 1stPlace in Romance/Science-Fiction and 2nd Place in Science-Fiction/Aliens &Alien Invasion in the Spring Bookfest Awards with her novel *Beyond The Steps of Stone*.

Beth holds a masters in English and Creative Writing and enjoys horseback riding, swimming, reading, cuddling her cats, and helping other authors hone their craft.

ALSO BY BETH A. FREELY

Novels

Behind The Eyes Of Dorian Gray
The Legend Of Captain St Pierre
The Loch
Beyond The Steps Of Stone
The Perfect Mix
Seduced By The Billionaire

BETH A. FREELY

Story Stories/Novellas

Memoirs of a Pomsky
A Taste Of Nostalgia
Brace For Impact
Letters From St. Nick
One Heated Night

About The Tainted Professors

Suits, ties and alibis.

These Professors are the ones your mama warned you about. Don't let their smart minds, quick whit or sweet faces fool you. Under the suit and calm demeanor is someone dying to show you how blissfully sinful they can be.

The Tainted Professors Series will leave you breathless, wanting—needing more.